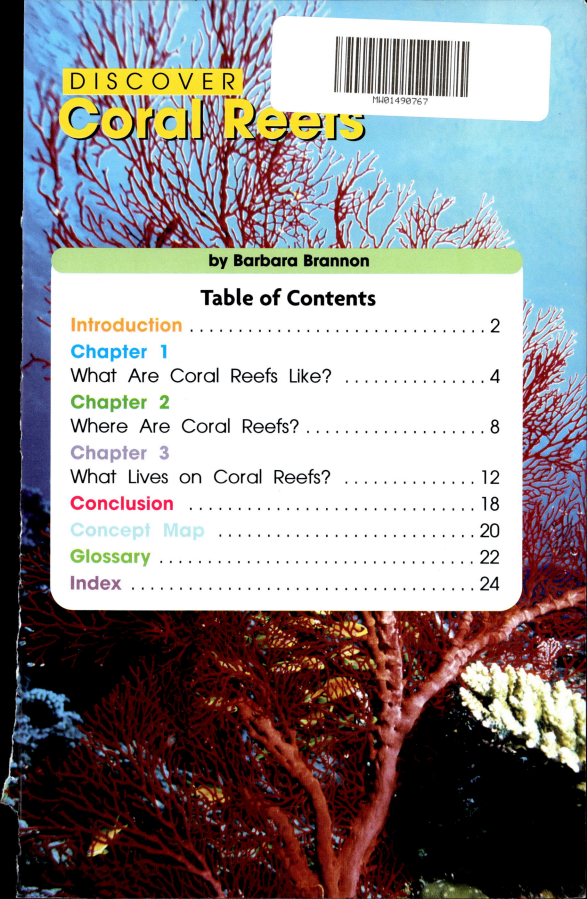

# DISCOVER
# Coral Reefs

by Barbara Brannon

## Table of Contents

Introduction . . . . . . . . . . . . . . . . . . . . . . . . . . . 2

**Chapter 1**
What Are Coral Reefs Like? . . . . . . . . . . . . . . 4

**Chapter 2**
Where Are Coral Reefs? . . . . . . . . . . . . . . . . . 8

**Chapter 3**
What Lives on Coral Reefs? . . . . . . . . . . . . . 12

Conclusion . . . . . . . . . . . . . . . . . . . . . . . . . . 18

Concept Map . . . . . . . . . . . . . . . . . . . . . . . . 20

Glossary . . . . . . . . . . . . . . . . . . . . . . . . . . . . 22

Index . . . . . . . . . . . . . . . . . . . . . . . . . . . . . . 24

# Introduction

Coral are small **animals.**
**Coral reefs** are many coral.

▲ Many coral form
coral reefs.

al are small sea animals.

# Words to Know

animals

coral reef

ocean

plants

salt water

sea

**See the Glossary on page 22.**

3

# Chapter 1

# What Are
# Coral Reefs Like?

Coral reefs are solid. Coral reefs are in **salt water**.

▼ Some coral reefs look like rocks.

Coral reefs are big. Coral reefs are small.
Coral reefs are in salt water.

▲ Some coral reefs are big.

▲ Some coral reefs are small.

Coral reefs are in clean water. Coral reefs are in salt water.

▲ Coral reefs grow in clean water.

Coral reefs are colorful. Coral reefs are in salt water.

▲ Coral reefs are full of color.

# Where Are Coral Reefs?

Coral reefs are in the Atlantic **Ocean**.

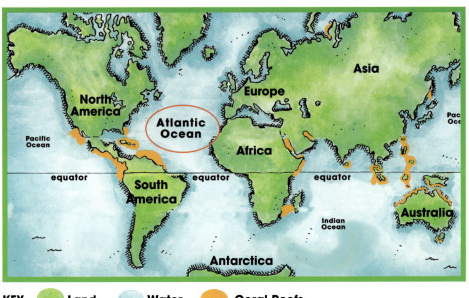

KEY　Land　Water　Coral Reefs

▲ This coral reef is in the Atlantic Ocean.

Coral reefs are in the Pacific Ocean.

▲ This coral reef is in the Pacific Ocean.

Coral reefs are in the Indian Ocean.

▲ This coral reef is in the Indian Ocean.

Coral reefs are in the Caribbean **Sea**. Coral reefs are in the Arabian Sea.

▲ This coral reef is in the Caribbean Sea.

▲ This coral reef is in the Arabian Sea.

# What Lives on Coral Reefs?

Animals live on coral reefs. Fish live on coral reefs.

▲ **Many ocean fish live on coral reefs.**

Shrimp live on coral reefs. Crabs live on coral reefs. Lobster live on coral reefs.

▼ This crab lives on a coral reef in Australia.

▲ This cleaner shrimp lives on a coral reef.

▲ This lobster lives on a coral reef in Micronesia.

Octopuses live on coral reefs. Squid live on coral reefs.

▲ Can you find the octopus in this picture?

▲ Can you find the squid in this picture?

Sponges live on coral reefs. Worms live on coral reefs.

▲ These sponges live on coral reefs.

▲ This worm lives on a coral reef.

15

**Plants** live on coral reefs. Grasses live on coral reefs.

▲ These plants live on coral reefs.

▼ These grasses live on coral reefs.

# Conclusion

▲ Coral reefs are colorful.

All coral reefs are in salt water. All coral reefs are full of life.

▲ Plants and animals live on coral reefs.

# Concept Map

Coral

plants

grass

# Reefs

## animals

- crab
- fish
- lobster
- octopus
- shrimp
- sponge
- squid
- worm

21

# Glossary

**animals** living things that can move from place to place

*Coral are **animals**.*

**coral reef** a water home for plants and animals

*Fish live on a **coral reef**.*

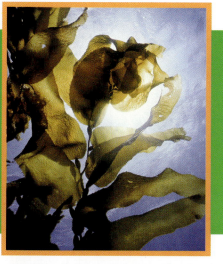

**ocean** a large body of salt water

*Coral reefs are in the Pacific **Ocean**.*

**plants** living things that can grow on coral reefs

***Plants** live on coral reefs.*

**salt water** water in the ocean

*Coral reefs are in **salt water**.*

**sea** a body of salt water

*Coral reefs are in the Arabian **Sea**.*

# Index

animals, 2–3, 12, 19

Arabian Sea, 11

Atlantic Ocean, 8

Caribbean Sea, 11

coral reefs, 2, 4–17, 19

crabs, 13

fish, 12

grasses, 16–17

Indian Ocean, 10

lobster, 13

Pacific Ocean, 9

plants, 16, 19

ocean, 5, 8–10, 12

octopuses, 14

salt water, 4–7, 19

sea, 2, 11

shrimp, 13

sponges, 15

squid, 14

worms, 15